People and Politicians
on the Way from Modernity to Contemporary Communality.
(2019)

*

essay

*

Traumear

People and Politicians
on the Way from
Modernity to Contemporary Communality

Generally, when we let our mind stray in this particular direction and think of people and politicians, we have two camps in mind plus some sort of a relationship of the two. People think of the country they occupy but politicians have the 'bigger picture' in mind. They think in terms of nation and state. So when people and politicians try to have a conversation, it turns out most peculiar at times – largely because they seem to speak a different language. Under the circumstances, this is hardly surprising. We come across a similar relationship when we look at the way teachers and pupils get along, or wholesalers and retailers, employers and employees. This is how the world seems to operate. We don't question it. We can see the dividing-lines and we try to operate along those lines. The modern world, however we look at it and approach it, exists as two halves and as various attempts to deal with the problems that arise due to this division. When we step back a bit we might ask: Is this the way it has always been? What about the ancient Greeks? The ancient Romans and the ancient Egyptians? Then we might think of the origin and development of democracy. Was that a way of spreading the responsibility somewhat, like the jury system in courts of law? The ruler says to the people: "Here, why should I take all the blame for bad decisions. Make up your own minds about what you want and maybe we can arrive at a compromise."

Then the modern world is born and instead of a god dictating from above through his chosen vessel, such as a holy priest or an anointed king, the people learn to speak up for themselves and the modern system comes into being. When it breaks down due to difference of opinion, force takes over for a while, in terms of some dictator, military or otherwise. Such dictators should not be confused with tyrants because tyrants exist pre-democracy. Once democracy has come into being there is no going back to tyranny, only to dictatorship. Like in a family – finally, when all the 'whys' have been asked, the head of the family says: Because I say so, basta. There's an end of it. For better or worse, there has to be order. It's the order of the modern world too. By hook or by crook, this order will assert itself, be it through means amenable or means drastic.

*

So the modern world, we might say, is systematic. Rules and regulations are both necessary and unavoidable. We try to understand this and to go along with it, to the best of our ability and good will but that does not mean we have to like it. We can imagine better. That's the trouble. We can imagine better. It's also a saving grace, that we can imagine better, because better is gradually becoming available. The modern world is not the only one we can imagine. There are others. Especially there is the world of the contemporary community and for the last fifty years or so this world seems to be drawing more and more attention to itself. Is it systematic? No, I don't think so. It draws attention to itself in a variety of ways, two of which, to my mind, seem to stand out. There is the way it challenges the status quo – we have had that before, to be sure. And there is the way it draws solutions to problems 'out of itself'; that we have not had before. It's new. Really we should say that it challenges the status quo by the way it draws solutions to problems out of itself rather than out of thin air or out of a selfish ego – or let's say out of tradition. Also observe the nature of the challenge. Is it the way of: Do it my way or I'll kill you? No, it's more a case of: 'Look at this! How about this! What do you think of this?' As for the origin of it – if I may sing the praises of it for a little while without getting down to specifics – the origin is not ideas and idealism but fellow feeling and communal thought. At the risk of sounding pretentious I would say that people are considering the distinct possibility of getting together while standing

2

on their own two feet. That would put paid to tribalism, and to the tribe, wouldn't it. – I shall try not to get ahead of myself.

Even as I speak (or write) I notice how the nature of the topic impresses upon me the need to consider both sides of the story – but within myself. Before I open my mouth I am obliged to think left and to feel right, or to feel left and think right – before I go on straight ahead. This creative union of thought and feeling is really the hallmark of contemporary community. The way *how* something is done is not only as important as *what* is being done but the two, in this case, are indistinguishable. I will come back again and again to this notion because it lies at the heart of my meaning here. Once one has stepped out of the modern system for the first time, one looks back and it almost seems like one has escaped from a trap. Very likely we have become involved in that system in a variety of ways and not everyone by any means escapes once and for all in every possible way. So what is required is numerous instances, over time, from a variety of traps. The systematic thinking and the systematic feeling, each separate from the other, has obliged us in many ways; we have formed many modern habits of thinking and feeling, all of which get in the way of contemporary community. We were like birds caught up in a net and the more we struggled, in terms of our modern techniques and schemes and methods, the more we became enmeshed. We have thoroughly tired ourselves out and we seriously wonder is there any way at all open to us if we want to continue.

However we cannot escape from the modern system by modern means. Surely that makes good sense. So here is the thing to do. Returning to the image of the trap: We keep our mind firmly on the truth that contemporary community is available for us and even influencing us and other than that we lie still in that trap and wait for it to open of its own accord. Which it will when the time is ripe. Contemporary community itself springs the trap for us.

Well, that is a way of looking at it. Let everyone come up with his or her own point of view. The modern system no longer works and that's a fact. Up to you how much frustration you still insist on experiencing before realization sets in. And it is frustrating, trying to escape from a sinking ship by clinging to the mast or by hoisting more and more sail. My heart goes out to you but you yourself are responsible for that initial change of heart. Or perhaps it should really be called a change of mind, because it is our mind, our opinions, beliefs and convictions that are caught up in these miserable states of being and to many of them we may be addicted. And while we are willing to die for them there is no help for us.

Mostly, I dare say, our case is not so desperate. Times have changed again. We are becoming more amenable to suggestions of how to leave the modern world behind and, by the way, without trying to make anyone else do it for us; even more important, without trying to force others to do it so that we don't have to bother.

*

Perhaps my wording is not at all apt here, when I say that we might choose to leave the modern world behind. The actual fact of the matter and the truth that would make us come to our senses is that the modern world is withdrawing from us. The modern world to begin with is the result of our anxiety about this and that and at the moment I cannot go into that, besides I have thoroughly gone into it elsewhere. What matters now and what we need to be honest with ourselves about is that the modern world system no longer works as the temporal assuagement of our anxiety. I believe we do well to look at the matter straight on. The modern system has been workable for a time, for two millennia, to be precise, and during that time those who had what it took to deal with their cosmic-metaphysical-personal anxiety properly rather than fearfully, in modern worldly terms, might go ahead and do just that. And they have done just that, here and there. Some of their works are available to us even today and much of their work was personally effective during their lifetime. If we look into their available works we find here and there sensible suggestions of why the modern world-systematic process cannot last and is not meant to last. But that is bye the bye. What we need to guard against is the unfortunate wishful thinking that if only we play our modern cards right we can make the system last. What is required and what will actually work is something else altogether, namely a getting ready for contemporary communality. How this plays out in terms of 'people and politics' specifically, that is what interests me here and what I hope to describe in this little essay.

Also, as the modern way of life becomes less effective, there are those who, out of whatever misguided anger or despair, make efforts to destroy it. However the modern system is not the sort of thing one can destroy. It contains even in itself all humanly available means of such destruction, so that we cannot step out of it with a view of dismantling it. That sort of anarchy, let me put it this way, is itself a modern concept. So is chaos. What can be destroyed, I suppose, or at least effaced, are the coincidental effects of modern progress – however what would be the point of that? Changing the map will not alter the country it represents. What we can do, and need to do, is manage the change-over and identify the transfer of power.

* *

This might in fact be a good way to begin, by realizing that there is no longer any such thing as political power. There are only degrees of effectiveness. What is, in fact, more or less powerful – powerful in the sense of being able to achieve some good – is how those who are in the know do, to some degree, steer that effectiveness, either *attractively*, in ways that will help to disabuse people of their desperate faith in modern methods and ways, or in the *direction* of greater insight in, and perception of, the time that is upon us.

5

A current politician, by which I mean someone who is 'in politics' at the moment but feels inclined in the direction of communality instead of statecraft, will already be effective by dint of being a politician. We do not have to wait until he behaves and does and acts before we appreciate him. His position alone makes him effective and he knows it. This allows us to speak of a positive communal-political tendency – positive in terms of transition. What he envisions as his task and purpose is transition from clandestine modernity to evident contemporary communality. Any useful policies he promulgates will help us, the people, to envision and fall in line with the very changes we ourselves feel urged to undergo in ourselves. So we may think of a kind of current politics – as still somewhat embedded in vestigial modern politics – as the outward, empirical image of the very change that also challenges, rationally, us as inhabitants of our country.

A current politician, rather than a modern one, evaluates the status quo of the population for which he is responsible and undertakes to facilitate that population's transition, in any and every way possible, to awareness of contemporary community – and, of course, to all the benefits incurred by such awareness. Since contemporary community is not a state but a way of life – for some even *the* way of life – the idea of 'status quo' will, in the meanwhile, lose all meaning. So, and in the same way, will the idea of statehood disappear. Remember that one is *conscious* of 'states of being' (a self-contradictory term) but one is *aware* of 'being in a state' and wanting out of it. In the same way, though more specifically, we can say that it is individuals who prefer static conditions – sadly individualists thrive on them – while individual persons value change and growth.

*

It must seem obvious from what we have learned so far that any politician, to be effective politically, will acquaint himself with what, for the lack of a better word, I will call the spirit of the time. Not of the times but of the time. This is what we describe when we speak of the decline of modernity and of the increased availability of contemporary community. As people we have the choice to fade away along with modernity or to rise to the occasion of contemporary community. We do well to believe that the spirit of the time favours the latter choice. This spirit is, after all, not a mythic invention but an aspect of good spirit, and in cooperation with good spirit we acquaint ourselves with true reality. So the spirit of the time is not a blind force. We believe it to our advantage. In collaboration with it we, already as current politicians, shape our policies to suit those, in particular, for whom we make ourselves responsible.

So in order to be able to 'read' the spirit of the time, we have to believe – or at least to assume – that this spirit 'is' and that it will cooperate with us to our benefit and advantage as we decide to move in the direction of contemporary community. Unless we introduce ourselves creatively into this stream of evolutionary growth, we fall by the wayside.

*

It comes down, in the end, to a way of seeing. If I put myself forward as someone who wishes to be and act as one of the caretakers of some particular country, I must have a pair of eyes, a capacity of vision that reveals to me how people, at any given time, *are* in relation to how they *might be*. This is an impressive formula. It would impress itself upon me as I move among people, as I observe them and converse with them. It would not be so much a case of listening to complaints and demands; there is much more to a conversation than that. An aspect of my caretaking would initially be how I present myself and how I let people know who I am and how I think and feel, in myself and for them, and if anyone were to misunderstand my position as caretaker I would wish to correct that.

So a primary task of a current politician would be to make as clear as possible that he is not a magician nor a mighty leader, nor, for that matter, simply someone who follows a party line and thinks in terms of government policy, but rather one of those people whose welfare he has at heart. Constant and repeated assurance of that would be given. The spirit of the time is the leader. Political wisdom resides in it. The politician is not in power or out of power but more or less clued in to that wisdom, depending on how much and how well he cares about the welfare of the population. Political wisdom is not learned at some institution but by concourse and intercourse with people.

And let's not make a thing out of 'the people'. Intellectuals produce myths and a politician has to leave those alone. There is no law against making a science out of whatever we come across on the earth but such sciences have nothing to do with the day to day lives of people. Often they are merely modern obstructions to keep the truth at bay. However there is a law against being unscrupulously selfish and it resides in the collective **temper** and **mood** of any population. No laws need to be passed to keep selfishness in check but something entirely different needs to be done, namely the collective temper and mood of the population needs to find expression and to be afforded means of expression. Immediately one thinks of 'the media'; of newspapers, radio, television, Facebook etc. These, however, are mostly modern stopgaps which at best can be relied on to highlight abuse. Also it would be wrong to equate the mood and temper of a population with 'the will of the people'. This 'will of the people' is nothing more than yet another reflection of the modern duality that afflicts us if we are not careful. Mood and temper is growth-related. Does a population grow? Surely only in number. And yet already the transition from modern to contemporary is akin to growth and on the way to real growth. We cannot speak of maturity here but definitely of an increasing sense of community and, for one example, of an awareness that decency, honesty and mutual assistance will replace their negative opposites.

The modern attempt to produce community is called communism. In use and effect it makes the point nicely that ethical behaviour cannot be instituted and enforced governmentally but that it has to be taught freely by personal example. So we may find that a population has suffered damage due to communism or due to capitalism, both of which are modern survival reactions. When a people governs itself and hopes to continue to do so now in terms of a tendency in the direction of contemporary community rather than on the basis of static, mutually contradictory values – which is no basis at all – it has to take account of how it has allowed itself to be damaged. In such a case, a population gradually changes from a perceived mass of unpredictable and largely unaccountable individuals to an actual number of responsible persons who eventually seek contact with other populations, again for the purpose of contemporary communality. At such a time a population becomes aware of its ethnic roots – if it has any.

Now ethnicity reminds us of nation and of nationality – but perhaps it does so mainly etymologically. Nations come and go but what about folk heritage? If a nation spreads out over several adjacent countries and attempts to accommodate these to its own national interests and characteristics – forcing them to learn its language, for but one example, then the folk heritage of those countries does not necessarily die but it may become recessive – and perhaps surface again once the conquering nation has died the death that must be the end all such ephemeral constructions. I am looking ahead here, in the direction of the contemporary communality that will eventually be earth-wide. Those who study these movements historically of peoples in the past, do it for other reasons altogether – perhaps they do it scientifically.

So when a current politician acquaints himself with a population he looks for remnants of nationality such as ethnic self-consciousness, for live or recessive folk culture and for the general mood and temperament of the people.

Nationality can be seen as an umbrella concept that encompasses a variety of phenomena. Some operate like tribal taboos, others like nostalgic reminders of past successes and tragic defeats. When nations in the past clashed with nations, some people stood aside and let them get on with it and behaved as they would if a pointless struggle broke out among individuals, over an insult or a slight. Nations declare war for survival reasons too, or they limit themselves to the strategic warfare of peacetime by undermining, humiliating and disturbing other nations, for material gain or for imposing their own religion or political creed. Individuals do the same. Corporations behave like nations, and here too, when money runs out, muscle takes over.

We cheer up, therefore, when we learn that even at a time when a population is still being governed as though it were a nation, a current politician is nonetheless able to make contemporary decisions without running foul of the pervading system. This is because from a national point of view, contemporary decisions are simply not understood – or somewhat understood and right away favoured. Also, it is not a contemporary policy or decision if it is intended as a reaction to, or contradiction of, any national ambition or measure. Just as a mature human being approaches an immature one with compassion while setting examples of maturity, in the same way does the contemporary politician behave towards national interests and conceits and those who would further them or embrace them. At times it must seem nigh impossible to get to the bottom of why people favour one kind of policy rather supporting another. All the same, in government as in the community, dire consequences are visited upon those who resist evil.

Contemporary communality is special, exceptional and exemplary. It works benignly both within a population and in government on behalf of a population. Current politicians do not speak a language that is different from that of the population for which they hold themselves responsible. They are not in any danger of hypocrisy or condescension. How interesting that the concepts of private and public gradually lose their meaning! People who favour contemporary community vote for politicians who suppose they can steer a government in that direction by making communal policies attractive and acceptable. Our best way of understanding this relies on our ability to think and feel outside the modern-systematic box. Imagine a prime minister who oversees a government manned entirely by current politicians. He would be able to take for granted that the population, on a majority basis, no longer has any interest in competing with nations of the world for so-called leadership of the world – absurd as that sounds in any case – and that communal measures could be openly discussed and put in motion. This government would then, probably for the first time in history, be able to concentrate primarily on quality of life and only secondarily on quantity of so-called goods, in the knowledge that the former does not depend on the latter. However as soon as quality of life is of primary importance, government as such does, to that extent, becomes less relevant. Quality of life depends each time on the person and not on the party, to put it succinctly. We have to search within ourselves for what would do us good. Each person would come up with a unique point to ponder and considering the origin of those points, soon a lively exchange would take place. People would discuss what they are for, not what they are against.

*

People do not have to be told by politicians what is good for them. They might forget for a while, when they become enamoured of some charismatic charlatan's promises but sooner or later they come to their senses and then maybe they string the fellow up. But politicians are themselves people and their experience of the modern world is as much under threat as that of every population across the earth nowadays. It is interesting when we see how some modern politicians view their state of nation as their own back yard; as for them to do with as they please. They pride themselves on having been voted into office because this gives them a mandate to do as they see fit. Perhaps we should admire them because after all they know what they are doing and why they do it, even though we see how their efforts at manufacturing a grand political state – the way an entrepreneur accumulates his millions – costs millions their livelihood and depletes the organic earth. Sooner or later people everywhere will say: It's our earth, not his! We all live on the earth and no longer in fenced-off plots of land where we feel obliged by Who-knows-who to give a quantifiable account of ourselves. And then they learn that they have to limit themselves, not others. It seems that certain forms of evil have to take their course and the smart man sees to his soul until the storm has blown over.

It is not an image of an ideal of peaceful co-existence that interest us here but a way out of the modern world. We believe that this escape from modernity is possible not by indulging in sentimental or violent idealism devised by modern thinking or feeling, but by describing for ourselves, from within ourselves, a believable modus vivendi based on political wisdom and wise politics. We call this way of life contemporary and communal because we believe that the time is ripe for it and that essentially it amounts not to selfish acquisition but to mutual care. That much we take as our starting point. The details need to be worked out. They need to be worked out on the ground, not in the abstract mind of a scientist. Different populations will work the details out in their own way and they will learn from one another, because they choose to be in touch. These details depend on the climate, on the earth environment and on the character and make-up of the people. Also there is no need to depend on land borders for a people to define itself, as long as by 'a people' we mean a communally minded population of some area, perhaps within still established state- or nation borders or even across such borders. The fact that such a communally minded, contemporary people cannot possibly fall into dispute or competition with state- or nationhood helps to define it. As soon as a quarrel arises between a contemporary and a modern population, the contemporary one will immediately discern an opportunity for popular growth.

This concept of popular growth is important and has to be looked at more precisely. The growth we imply here is that of **indigenous cohesion** and **exigent effectiveness** – in other words, the very opposite of a political party, which demands loyalty to a creed and which is about as effective as circumstances allow. Actually the comparison is not worth much to start with. What we are contemplating might be the population of a country and what we mean by a country does itself have to be looked at in detail. When victorious nations get together and carve up a strip of territory into parcels to which none of the nations object too much, those parcels are not countries, nor are they likely ever to turn into countries, because warring tribes have at least some sort of cohesion and they will not be checked by vicariously drawn lines on a map. Against that, if due to one man's calculating bloody-mindedness a lot of 'lands' are joined up artificially under one convenient label so as to thwart some imaginary aggressor, the outcome may be rampant nationalism but again, nothing that is organically essential. The nations of the earth, by and large, are cobbled-together in the interest of greed and creed, not naturally occurring populations. The United Kingdom of Great Britain and Northern Ireland, for one example, is so sick and tired of its assumed responsibilities, it would gladly revert to just being Great Britain, as a first step. Then it turns out that Welsh, Scottish and English are names that have far more real meaning than British, and this is because these three are at least countries, whereas 'Britain' is a label for a nation.

We band together in fear. We invent a European Union out of fear. This is the typical modern fear that initially crops up within each individual and its true purpose is to draw his attention to creative work that is possible here and needs to be done so that we may turn into responsible persons. The modern reaction is to shrug off the responsibility and to project the fear outside onto some enemy whom we produce ourselves for that nefarious purpose. When a member of the club (the United Kingdom? Scotland?) decides to go it alone again, the ancient panic surfaces and the media descend into furies of agitated babbling.

One might like to compare this to what goes on when a child grows up and leaves the nest, but that in itself is a natural process and not to be meddled with. Mature understanding meets all the requirements. A nation, by comparison, is a child that refuses to grow up. It is an individual who will not turn into a responsible person. Its existence is based on arrogance and timidity. It's main and sole ambition is the preservation and prolongation, if necessary by force and violence but finally by whatever it takes, of its static existence. Exaggerated collective self-consciousness 'gives birth' to a nation, whereupon self-aggrandizement and delusional myths give berth to it – for as long as it lasts.

The population thrives and suffers or suffers and dies. It's meaningless to speak of the population of a nation. In reality a number of populations are to be identified in most nations. Each population has what it takes to grow, however this is difficult within the national compound. National interests are geared to override popular growth. The word 'popular' has itself, under nationalist pressure, come to mean 'liked by many people', which is something else entirely.

By the **indigenous cohesion** of a population we mean mutual recognition in terms of **mood** and **temperament**. One can imagine how this grows, and why it can grow, as soon as political acknowledgment takes time and place and while political awareness and cooperation are brought into the light of day. What is implied by this, in the end, is that people act on their political understanding in terms of mutual recognition while avoiding like the plague any and all demonstration, literally of anything, in public. Again, any attempt to indulge in such demonstration merely highlights then the need for inward regeneration. After all, the separation of private and public and of private from public has no meaning in the case of genuine, contemporary population.

What does have meaning – and meaning is always crucial when it comes to our sharing with others our wishes and preferences – is courage and cowardice, indifference and attitude, inanition and transcendence. This is the sort of meaning against which contemporary people test their grasp of reality and their appetite for change in growth. Since our image of any thriving population in community demands that we take it seriously, we are equally obliged to make ourselves, as people of a population, accessible to other populations. This eager readiness to relate to other populations is an important element of population growth. As a matter of fact, we in our political population will either seek to be open to communication and to communicate or else we will find ourselves becoming complex instead of simple. The onset of complexity should right away persuade us to reach out to other populations. The onset of complexity is right away systematic and tempts the population to arrogate to itself all sorts of rights and rituals that will make it stand out and seek identity. If others identify and label it now, this will hopefully be noticed and interpreted correctly as a step in the wrong direction. It will appear to uninvolved people that this population longs to return to modernity, so right away they will involve themselves and offer assistance, either by adopting that population and amalgamating with it or merely by standing by and protecting it against further misfortune.

All this will be done politically, which is to say by creating a position for someone from that population who will moderate and govern while policies are structured, plans are discussed, options for action are suggested, debated and adopted or rejected. The position for a moderator or the like is created anew each time there is a call for political action.

*

This might be a good place to think about what exactly I meant by political action. One serious question has to be, is it action at all? I am not concerned with the modern version now. In the contemporary realm, when people realize they are up against a dilemma that concern them all in one way or another, they cannot very well roll a die an let it choose one of six options for them. No, someone has to be selected as a figure head, a person who can be respected and who is able to be a focus of attention. Really what goes on then is a sort of discharge of energy from a higher power which can now be imagined on account of this popular configuration. One agrees to participate in a play and to be a member of the audience at the same time. A most peculiar energy is released. And this energy comes in very handy because it heightens and intensifies how everyone experience what is going on. Or imagine a group of people who are distressed and confused over something unfamiliar. They suddenly begin to argue with one another, to accuse one another, then they apologize and express feelings of despair. Now it occurs to someone to isolate himself from the rest a little so that that he can make a suggestion that promises to clear the air for everyone. They look to him with hopeful expectation. Something is happening here that has a political dimension to it. There is pointed concentration, there is a division of a mass into two which is followed by attempts to make the two one. Compared to a play, this is reality because it is shaped. One should not try

16

to imagine again now someone who might be observing this and forming opinions on it. No, it is the final, universal or cosmic, shape of reality so far as people and populations are concerned and it takes places under no one else's eyes. Not even God is watching, because god is utterly involved in it. We should not hesitate to speak of the spiritual dimension of every contemporary political process. The entire population may well be aware of it and in that case one could speak of communality in action. And it all goes on out in the open, in the light of day, not in people's minds.

This is of course the essential characteristic of contemporary political effectiveness, that one can point it out to one another and say: Look, we are involved in a political struggle and nothing is hidden from us and at the same time good spirit is active on our behalf. Surely we are fortunate to be able to behave like this. It is once again time for our population to increase. Let us be glad and grateful. The spirit of the time is upon us and we do not shirk our duty. We have chosen someone to focus our attention and he has agreed to perform in this role of moderator and facilitator. Now for a time whatever comes up in our various verbal contributions will right away be joined by some seemingly opposing or diametrically different contribution. One of us will say: We should invite some skilled people from this neighbouring population to show us how to go about this or that. Then another will say: Let us not invite them but offer them a large gift if they are willing to help us. And a third someone will come out with: We can surely manage the first half ourselves and only then we ask for advice, because in this way we will learn new skills, even from our mistakes. And so on. Egotism is not involved. No one insists on being in the right or on having the only possible solution to some problem. No one comes up with an idea that will sort the difficulty. Really there is no difficulty. There is no problem. What there is can only be described as an opportunity for contemporary communal growth and if there is talk of bridges over streams, of scrubland to be cleared or of tempestuous youth to be disciplined, then that is symbolic content that must not be taken too seriously.

When a married couple suddenly finds itself at loggerheads after a lengthy period – let's say a number of weeks – of affection, mutual understanding and trust, the husband will not try to enforce his opinion and the wife will not state her rights so that one might even then speak of divorce proceedings, but they both understand that the time has come for a strengthening of their bond and therefore of the increased capacity for life of each. I did not call them a modern couple. They will both, individually, appreciate the value of suffering any pain that comes along with interruption of mutual affection. That's the first reminder. Then each will realize that the other is suffering and will therefore care more about the suffering of the other than his or her own. This creative compassion eases the influence of new life. There might be some half-serious fighting but each secretly wishes the other well rather than concentrating on self-pain. Each realizes that this is going to take time, 'like all good things'. If they separate and go into different rooms then this is only so that they can collect their wits more successfully so as to be able to renew their love.

That is how life-growth works. In the case of the married couple it makes no sense to speak of political process because there is no population. Nonetheless in the case of both the population and the married couple there is life-growth because modernity has been scuttled by the way the ground has been cleared for marital love here and for popular communality there.

*

This 'clearing of the ground' would be the initial ambition of the up-and-coming politician who has a 'nose for the times'. He looks around carefully and detects cracks in the walls here and there that are not readily papered over. He may decide that something is to be done along the ethical frontier. Instead of defining ethical behaviour as various attempts to remain within the social borders of moral acceptability, he will search within himself for ways of introducing small reminders here and there of what it means to be a human being – namely someone who looks to his own inner soundness rather than to external 'fashionability' in his dealings with others. In the meantime he intuits the 'coming reality'. Right away, as we mentioned earlier, due to the fact that he is someone in the interest of the contemporary spirit, even before he says or does anything he creates a communal affinity – which opens helpful doors and closes others to hindrances. At the risk of 'romantics' one might observe that in the absence of the likes of such communal affinity – which from without is often taken for personal charm – nothing of value in the direction of contemporary politics can really be made to work. On the other hand, things turn good contrary to all expectations where this affinity operates. Think of it simply as soul in operation. The modern soul, by comparison, is really a psyche, which cannot sustain the fluctuations of personal or political life-growth but it collapses under it and before it. Meanwhile it does its best to belittle and shame soul-operation in those who practice it, *so that*, as seen sub-specie-aeterni, soul does not remain a mere sensation of a capacity but either learns to sustain and propound itself or else it turns into regret and disrepute.

The onus is therefore on the politician who wishes to be contemporary to nourish this ethical affinity within himself as a way of 'clearing the ground' for what can then be brought to his doorstep by the contemporary spirit of the time.

They will not be ideas that he will 'have'. Let him not look for ideas that will allow him to energize his day. Ethical affinity at the beginning leads to ethical behaviour. The modern politician will always draw a line between his private life and his public duties, so that how he behaves in private should have no bearing on his political work. Then the modern public will seek to bring him down because he will not behave ideally also in private. On the other hand we have to keep in mind that the ethical affinity and the very definition of ethical behaviour of the contemporary politician bears a different stamp from the ethics of modernity. Contemporary ethics is and remains a personal secret. One does not discuss it with others and it is not 'preachable'. One knows that one's integrity depends upon it. Although it eventually relies upon a growth-factor of its own – in the beginning, so that it may, so to speak, come into its own, the meaning of **honour** and **nobility** will have to be entertained by the prospective politician. In the absence of these his ethical soul will not thrive and his contemporary ambitions – they probably will be ambitions rather than aims in that case – will fail.

To the modern mind honour and nobility are large words which imply, especially nowadays, almost impossible efforts at moral respectability. One avoids them to avoid being pompous. A contemporary politician, by comparison, will quickly learn that the seeds for honourable behaviour and noble doing are to be found in his ethical affinity, which is to say in his very 'being for others'. Consequently he will never have to put himself forward for candidacy to a post as a modern politician would, because his calling little by little becomes obvious to many in his population – especially to those who are fed up with the modern duplicity and the never-ending 'scrabbling up the cursus honorum'.

The seeds are there, in his inner sanctum, and of course they have to die, as they will under the initial onslaught of modern resentment and criticism. Our politician will not resist these evils, for he knows what is good for him and he understands how he will make marvellous headway while he absorbs these resentments and criticisms and especially while he does so gladly. Indeed why would he not do so gladly if I knows that he is doing himself some major good?

*

So what we need to find out now is how, initially, our politician might be honourable and noble. We know that he functions from within, not in relation to private or public concerns. How might he feel, if he were suddenly to decide to respond honourably, for example? It might, for example, come to his attention that someone is being treated shamefully. Someone has taken advantage of someone's weakness, in order to aggrandize himself. Our politician takes note of the anger rising in himself and views the bigger picture. He realizes that the perpetrator of the outrage is to be pitied, while the shamed person is in need of compassion. One notes that no rejection of evil is involved, and this is of crucial importance if honour is to play a role. At the same time the politician will wish to do something. He wants to act, to do some good. His ethic affinity is alive in him now. The seed has sprouted. What he cannot and will not do is act by rote or according to some trivial policy. It does not occur to him to ask: "How does one behave under such circumstances? What can I get away with? What will happen if I do such and such?" Why does this not occur to him? Or why, as soon as it does, does he right away remove his consciousness of it? Because he knows that the appropriate response will occur to him only if he waits for it to come to him from the direction of good spirit. This is what it means to be honourably passionate. He is passionate not for his own sake but for someone else. It is an honourable move, that he does not perform reactively but instead he placed himself at the mercy of good spirit within him.

Eventually it occurs to him what to do. However, although now he knows, he still has not done. He has allowed good spirit to inform him, as it were; to condition him in the right direction and to make the appropriate action appear attractive. We can with confidence say that what he will do will be done nobly, because he will invariably be offering and giving of his life.

Here we have honourable behaviour and noble doing in a nutshell. Something that becomes simple and straight forward due to practice seems complicated only because it has to be described in terms that will set it apart from modern superficiality and indifference. How can every contemporary political decision be made? Honourably and nobly. Familiarity with good spirit, which began as a nodding acquaintance with the spirit of the time, gradually increases with such being, doing and behaving. And since all contemporary political action is appropriate, we understand now how this works.

When we say that a contemporary politician is passionate, we mean this ability and willingness of his to treat the one who is wrong and the one who is right with equal respect; to pity the one who behaves badly and to be compassionate on behalf of the one who is being badly treated. That is really the beginning of good action – which cannot fail, by the way. His appropriate political decisions are arrived at in this manner. He will soon discover that once he knows what to do, he still has to think about how he will do it. How will he present his decision and how will he execute it. That part of it will be nobly managed, because he will not leave it to others, he will not delegate and deny further responsibility, but he will let it be know that he is the one who is acting. When he does delegate, he inspires others to behave nobly, and they in turn will do the same.

What we need to realize is that what is appropriate will not necessarily appear to be appropriate. However we can be absolutely certain that if the decision is arrived at nobly and honourably, the action must be appropriate, however it appears.

When we concentrate on being right and on doing the right thing, we behave in accordance with presupposition and preordination – in other words, we keep an eye on law. We behave consciously and are guided by conscience. We may well end up having done the right thing, which judgment we might be able to defend more or less successfully, however we will not be capable of excellence and of the higher perfection – which shape every truly appropriate action.

If the political action is appropriate, it promotes contemporary community – not at the expense of modern society but not in line with it either. Indeed, in case it should be necessary to repeat this, any attempt to 'deconstruct' modernity is pointless. Not only does the removal of modern myths facilitate in any way anything even vaguely to do with contemporary world, but such a removal, on close inspection, is not possible in any case. How would one go about it and remain honest? Nor, in third place, is any such removal necessary because modernity is removing itself in any case presently. The sooner we look in our inward human nature and search for the contemporary truth, the quicker will we learn the language that will suit us to construct, in our present case, a contemporary political approach to populations, especially those which still cling to statehood and entertain national ambitions.

Both the population and any prospective contemporary politician will gain from the likes of this present work in front of the reader here. It certainly helps if a population recognizes those who have the contemporary calling, so that it may accept them as guides, and those who have it are bound to benefit from works such as the present.

* *

I cannot help wondering what a contemporary politician would understand by the term 'policy'. "What is the Conservative Party's policy on immigration?" the modern politician might ask, and what he means is a complex of decisions that have been arrived at which will guide, at least until some change is made, that party's thinking and actions on the score of immigration. The contemporary politician would consider that it stops him from thinking. He would have to say: Whatever I

23

mean by immigration will have to fall into this predetermined category. No one will be allowed into the country unless they can help raise the level of the economy. A mechanism of screening has to be invented. A perpetual count of skills in the country will have to be kept up. Then he imagines meeting an immigrant at the border and saying to him: "I'm sorry but we don't need you. You cannot come in." That is all perfectly clear. No one would argue with the wisdom of it. He calls to mind, however, what the notion of an ever growing 'economy' really means. He will not shut his mind to that. Nations are in competition over who has the fastest growing economy. So the immigration policy is tied to this absurdity that encourages and justifies massive consumption by the population, that depletes and destroys the earth-environment and increases the gap between the rich and the poor in terms of property and quality of life. What is he to do?

It is not up to him to highlight the absurdity of a voracious type of survival. Others must do that. It falls to him to consider if he might suggest some other way of dealing with prospective immigrants. They are emigrating from their home country because they cannot fit into the system of their government and they choose to come to a country which is rightly or wrongly known to them as economically well developed. Who would blame them? There they stand at the door, in droves.

He hands his problem over as described in a previous section of this work. All the various pictures that offer to guide his thought are cleared. Soon he comes up with the notion that immigration is not the problem at all but division of labour. People want to sell their labour instead of applying it directly to their survival needs. They look for a job rather than doing the next thing that needs to be done in relation to their own existence.

Eventually he decides that he does not wish to be involved in any way with this immigration policy because he understands it as in effect touching on one of the many tragedies of modern existence. He might go so far as to devise measures for making immigrants who are being kept in holding centres as comfortable as possible. Beyond that sort of action he considers himself to be powerless. By withholding his involvement in the policy itself he makes a point – which at first he refuses to explain. He feels sorry for those who are involved in the tragedy. In other words he realizes that they are involved, really to the extent of any modern problem, in a process that depletes them and he wishes he could make them understand but he cannot. What he can do is help to minimize the fallout. That may not amount to much to the eyes of some, however the point he makes of refusing to agree or disagree with a modern policy may raise a relevant question here or there, and then he might explain himself. In that way he would be true to his contemporary being.

We have to keep in mind here that he is not a modern individual who has decided to adopt, for the time being, a few contemporary ideas. Neither is he contemporary in the sense that he thinks and behaves the way people tend to think and behave nowadays. He is contemporary in that he cooperates with good spirit here and now. He is also a politician in that he offers his thought and action to the population that would make use of it.

The two important concepts here are cooperation with good spirit and population. The meaning of the former is perhaps difficult to grasp by anyone who has no experience of good spirit but the meaning of the latter should be readily understandable to most people, since the population of a country means all the people who legally live in it. Mind you, since we are describing a period of transition in this work, we should not expect any particular term or concept, any name or label for that matter, to remain the same throughout.

*

Our human individuality, the individuality of every human being, is available for recognition to that particular human being and not to anyone else. My individuality is the way I perceive myself. Since human perception draws equally on outward and inward knowledge, I may develop an image of myself that combines my knowledge of how I think and feel, my insight into my emotion and temperament, with how I, in particular, experience my environment. My view of myself combines insight and experience. What I learn, as I mature, is that I change and that this change may be usefully and correctly viewed as growth. Both the change and the growth I may view from within and from without and of course by doing both I make sure that my intelligence remains whole.

Maturation implies the will to work and to create works. To that end a human being develops his personality. Works are outward creations. We can point them out to one another. Where? In the world here and now. A person presents his or her changing individuality to the world here and now as works. As a person I am aware of my individuality as productive and creative. I hold myself responsible for my individuality. Its organic potential, its various organic possibilities, are realized by me personally and presented to the members of my community – which is to say to those with whom I am in touch – but also freely to anyone who wishes to draw on them for benefit. What I mean by my community is crucial. It grows out of my willingness to be responsible for my individuality and on the basis of my works. By means of these works I communicate. They are my link with those who choose to respond to them. Every mature word I speak, if it is heard and responded to, builds community.

Now if I decide to keep my individuality to myself – which I am liable to do to the extent that I refuse to be responsible for it – I turn into an individual rather than becoming a person. At the same time, even though I have nothing to offer, I want to be noticed. This is the basic survival instinct coming to the fore, that I want to be noticed. I want others to point to me and say: That is what's his name, isn't it? If they keep forgetting my name I will gravitate in the direction of others who are equally in that predicament. We might get together and form a society, a club, a movement, and we will decide on a name for it – a label, really – and our survival instinct dictates that we should increase our membership as much as possible. Or, in the same interest of getting noticed, we keep the membership low and make up a select group, of which others will enviously take note.

Really this need to be noticed is what is left over from the responsible willingness to create works. I don't want to have the trouble of being responsible for myself but this does not mean that I want to disappear into my fruitless individuality. That would be insane. Excuse me. I have rights. I have as many rights as I can invent for myself in order to make the point that I too am here – and who knows, I may eventually become crea-tive, so do not entirely count me out. Besides, I am creative, in a peculiar way to be sure, in that I exhibit how I manage to be an individual, how I manage to reject the advances of personal-ity and any demands made on me to become responsible, and last but not least how I marshal my still available energies to resist and reject the never-ending threat of the chaos to which some refer as the elements. I may even turn into an individual-ist by insisting that my individuality is the only right and proper one and all the rest are sham.

Nations are built by individuals. Nationalism is a product of individualism. Individualists insist that their combined way of resisting the chaos and rejecting personal responsibility is the only 'true' one. No wonder nations are forever at one another's throats as they fight for hegemony in terms of whatever comes to hand, such as interpretation of origin, military prowess, and finally economic growth. Shall we say that if a nation chose to become responsible for itself it would turn into a decent country and forget about ruling the world? A bit far-fetched I suppose, but it makes a point.

Things get more interesting now when we glance at the population of a nation. On one hand there are those who keep the spirit of the nation alive and within bounds and those who forever insist on going to extremes: the individuals and the individualists. They 'understand' that we have to arm ourselves because of the enemy, but they don't understand that the enemy feels exactly the same way about them. The only alternative for them is allowing oneself to be taken over by the enemy. There is no knowledge whatsoever of 'love of enemy'.

On the other hand there are those who really have no interest in nation or in nationalism because they are happy to lead anonymous lives. They don't care to be singled out and it matters little to them that no one will point to them and say: "Ah, there goes a this or that!" If they want to raise a family they like to have enough food and shelter and it would never occur to them to think of themselves as rich or poor. As long as there is enough to go around. If the Catholics and Protestants, or the republicans and the royalists fight, they keep their heads down, their noses to the grindstone, and hope the nonsense will soon blow over. If cotton is cheaper than wool, they buy cotton but the children are taught to knit. If electricity comes along they use it but they keep candles on hand. If the only shops in the vicinity overload their shelves with mass-produced, plastic wrapped potatoes and cabbages they buy them but in the meantime they keep a kitchen garden going, just in case. They might vote in the next election but they admit they don't really know what it's all about. They rarely get carried away by propaganda. They are suspicious of the media. They listen politely to the Member of Suchandsuch at the door and then they invite the neighbour in for a chat and a cup of tea. They produce art in a small way. And they usually think of themselves as living in a community. They realize that you have to make an effort sometimes to keep community alive but they try not to make a thing out of it. Community is as natural as birth and death and one way to kill it off is to make a thing out of it – to study it, to analyze it, to try to produce it artificially. How foreign the idea of statehood is to them may be observed in the way they welcome the stranger, the oddball, the sick person, the cripple and the dwarf. They try to avoid social standards as much as they can, though at times they get infected a little and that usually leads to a row or two.

The danger with them is that they don't organize themselves, not as a group, oh no, but as individual people. They don't say to themselves, each in his or her own way: "I wonder why I'm around in the first place? Why am I occupying space on earth?" And why is this a danger? It leaves them open to criticism and the spirit of criticism is the modern spirit which hollows out whatever can be hollowed out. It seems we are not any longer just allowed to say: "I mind my own business and let the rest go hang." It never worked, but during the modern age – I mean the last two-thousand years – the reminders that people need to organize themselves have been getting stronger all the time. And when people resist this urge within them they allow themselves to be organized by others, as groups, for revolutions of one sort or another. The lesson there is: If you don't organize yourself you will get organized. In other words, you will be organized en masse because you don't organize your self. Notice I emphasize: your self, not yourself. There's a secret involved here which I refuse to draw out into the open for good reason.

The fact that we speak of 'people' is interesting in itself because we cannot speak of an individual one, the way we speak of an individual person. We have become accustomed to think of people en masse. Looking at one at a time is actually quite novel.

"People of the world unite!" The ideologues use people like bread dough and like cannot fodder. The sociologists study them and the socialists guide them – en masse. The religious leaders with the help of theology whip them up into a frenzy and set them at each other's throats. Two world wars and the various so-called holocausts have demonstrated where it all leads. That is not all that has been going on, not by any means, however it illustrates in the particular what happens when individual people do not organize themselves and as a consequence others organize them – and that means trouble. As for the great organizers themselves – well, what about the most recent ones, I mean Lenin and Stalin, Hitler, Mussolini and all the others which demonstrated so clearly what you can do with people if they don't organize themselves. We try to imagine them inclining with a pipe on their favourite chair, at the end of their life, as they look back on a productive life well spent – however we fail.

So how would people organize themselves – each one by him or herself? He would have to say to himself: I am tired of being pushed around. I am equally fed up drifting along as if I had no mind and heart of my own with which I might engage. So I will no longer allow myself to be seduced by the media or to be bullied by the State but I will think and feel for myself. I will educate myself. In other words I will, by hook or by crook, pull myself out of my stupor and learn to think for my self. It is my self that causes me problems and I shall take it in hand. My self is both a hindrance and a liability unless and until I take it in hand and give it some shape. I might go to night classes and learn from those who have already begun to do that sort of thing. My self will be the thing that I shall clean up and whip into shape until I can feel proud of it.

He would have to say that to his self and she would have to say to her self. For a while they would be minding their own business, strictly, that goes without saying. If you want to take your self in hand you have to pay attention exclusively to it for a while, while the boyfriend and the girlfriend, the wife and the husband, each mind their own serious business. After a while they will exchange notes. "Here, you know what I've discovered? It helps me to write a diary. It helps me to reflect on my self." "Really? What a good idea. That wouldn't work for me now. But I've decided to volunteer for that waste-management outfit that started last month. Also I'm able to do my housework more patiently." "That's great. Maybe we could go to that community play together. Would you like that? They're different plays, you know. Not just calculated to take our mind off our troubles."

Their self is the thing that wakes up and let's people know of its whereabouts. To the extent that they are not looking for it they are bound to experience various upsets and discomforts, maybe even illnesses of mind or body. Youngsters commit suicide because their self is drawing attention to itself and they do not know how to return the complement (sic). Even young men and women are liable to kill themselves for that reason, and those who have not yet heard of the awakening self are shocked, startled and dismayed. Let them look around. Let them learn from what is going on around them. The adults are so tied into their modern responsibilities – into their various flights from them – that their self barely occurs to them except as now and again a longing for rest and peace. Ease up on the hot whiskeys and the cannabis, I say, and look to your self.

The thing is, when you find it – or when it finally finds you – it does have a message. It will tell you the truth. Not the 'bare' truth, the 'naked' truth and the 'cruel' truth – those are for others to deal with, but the truth insomuch as it suits you here and now. So when you wonder what you should do now, while faced with this present confusion, overcome by this present grief or visited by so much happiness it frightens you a little, look to your self and a passage will open out of the dire straits and into helpful advice, into comfort or into reassurance – from your self.

After an unpredictable while you will look for your self and find something else, something rather wonderful, and I will not tell you right now what it is, lest you become impatient, but your self until then has, quite understandably, hidden it from view. Eventually, from looking at it and to it so often, your self will fade from view and then you will get a pleasant surprise. But more of that another time.

*

Now what is a contemporary politician to do and how is to be have in the light of the fact that a great section of the population he serves is caught up in ignorance of their self because they can think of nothing except themselves while another section is besieged by illnesses and problems and handicaps and griefs for no other reason than that they do not understand all these hindrances as good messages relating to the fact that their self is desirous of coming into its own but cannot because it is getting no attention at all from them in kind? Will he say: This has nothing to do with me. There are specialists and experts and professionals who deal with this and make it their problem. My task begins and ends with policies and policies relate solely to external matters such as defence and foreign affairs, with terrorism and immigration and that sort of thing. I am happy to make the odd speech and maybe give people a lift by pretending things are not as bad as they look but beyond that I much pretend to hand over to the priests and the ministers of the cloth, to the consultants, the clinicians and the general practitioners, the social workers and the psychiatrist, because they, after all, know these people in detail. (Oh, do they really?) They are able to work closely with them on a one to one basis whereas I am dealing with crowds, surely; with audiences – in other words with masses of people, not with individuals. There are the unemployed, the homeless, the students and the poor – and of course the rich and the taxpayers. Come to think of it, I am not really in touch with any humanity. Now why is that? I am in touch

32

with numbers but not with people. Statistics are my bread and butter. I argue with my colleagues about what I would be wise to say and what not to say because after all where democracy is concerned, the first thing is to get into office. If you're not in office you may have a heart of gold but no one will know you.

This makes me just a little uneasy, when I think of it like that. I mean one can pretend to care about the poor students and the exorbitant fees they have to pay, but one ought to care equally about the poor universities which barely seem to cope, with their watered-down curriculum that has to suit almost everyone these days, and their pay checks which are always too meagre. One can pretend to care, this is true, but it's a balancing act, isn't it, because whatever you give to the left you have to take away from the right, and vice versa.

Well, this particular politician seems in dire straits, mostly because he suffers from conscience. He checks with his colleagues and most of them, if he communicated his concerns, would sneer cynically and tell him to catch himself on. It's dog eat dog, mate, face it. Try not to read the papers. Forgive them, they all have to make a buck, like you and I.

He turns away, his conscience quiet for the moment. We're all in the same boat. Why should I make my life into a burden!

However it's his conscience that makes of his life a burden. Then he thinks about conscience. What is it. Why will it not go away and play dead. He rushes from task to task a little more hectically, but to no avail.

Really his conscience is his self. This he realizes now. It comes to him in his sleep. He wakes up, turns over, feels restless – gets up. In the middle of the night he gets up and thinks. He is on his way to becoming a contemporary politician. He is about to learn how to refer his cares to his conscientious self rather than to some external parameters that have been set up by those thousands of experts whose conscience has never gnawed at them. When he thinks about crime and refers it to itself – crime with its multitude of tentacles that reach deep into the bowels of modern society – he goes blank. Crime suddenly means nothing to him. And this is a good sign, for the moment, because for once he is not being badgered by a crowd of external details, none of which he can really do anything about because if he scratches here somewhere else will right away begin to itch and besides, scratching only makes it worse. So he perseveres with his self, even though it screams and kicks at first because it wants to be left to its own devices. Does it occur to him suddenly that he himself is a bit of a criminal? That he has only been lucky so far? Well, surely not. However he does feel inclined to think of the criminal as not merely a statistic. How strange. That had never occurred to him. These are people who are suffering the consequences of their unregarded conscientious self. In a sense, so is he. Is he in the wrong job? But surely anyone who does work would be smart to look for the down-to-earth connection between himself and others. How could a general practitioner in medicine afford to lose track of that connection? It would kill him. Surely they are never done making sure that their unconcerned self does not remain unconcerned for longer than it takes for them to feel the pinch of it? (Well, anyway, we hope so, don't we.)

Trust in politics is on his agenda now and he knows it. How can people trust politicians if politicians don't trust themselves? If they refuse to face their self so that they may ask it questions?

*

So how do we use the word politics now; and the word politician? What happens in our mind when we hear that someone has made a political decision? Weighing the pros and cons? The consequences? Surely we would rather not think of politics as a game. Not if it matters to us whether people are in pain or not. However what about 'the people'? I can come up with compassion for people, but 'the people' are really an entity onto themselves and more or less a mythic creation. "Power to the people!"

we hear the shouting in the city and we ask: Which people do they mean? Who are 'the people'? This is surely a mythic conception and right away is born that which vies with 'the people' for 'power', namely 'the government' and 'the politicians'.

Now we know what we are up against if we want to continue to think straight and compassionate. We are up against a complex of myths. We do well to keep our wits about us. The people do not really exist. People do, but not the people. Neither do the politicians exist, for the same reason that myths are not real. Are they momentary lapses of our critical faculties – I mean the faculties we need to identify a crisis and to find our way out of it on the side of reality?

Mind you, there is something that just loves myths and that is critical spirit. However what we need in order to be able to get out of a crisis is a critique, which involves sound judgment. Criticism, in comparison, takes us into the crisis and seeks to make us comfortable in it, in a self-serving kind of way. By way of criticism we do not exit from a crisis but we fudge it. We also complicate it endlessly and needlessly. And we perpetuate it. Criticism is a modern disease and modernity is its crisis. If we study modern history – not in the modern way, of course – over the past two millennia, what we look at is some of the ways people have dealt with myths – and how they have come up with them in the first place. A modern mind will look at everything and see myths. And a modern mind will not take kindly to being reminded of this.

*

Mythology, as the study of myth and of myths, can be quite interesting.[1] On account of the supernatural aspect of myths, if we employ them during argument we have to know what we are doing. If we speak to people who think mostly in terms of myths and we wish to influence their thinking in the direction of truth

---

[1] I refer the reader to my book: Mythology the Science of Myth.

35

a little, we might choose to speak in parables. A parable will allow a modern mind to concentrate upon its self a little while it refrains from confronting it with the truth; the truth would very likely drive it further into the supernatural realm of myths. It does not confront it with the truth, however it allows truth to shimmer through. In that way it is liable to create a taste for truth without causing a modernist reaction.

So what we are getting around to here is that if a politician wishes to be effective and not merely in a well-paid job he has to be able to tell a story, a good and useful story, in order to benefit those among his people whose minds are more accustomed to myths than to dealing with facts. Facts need to be approached with deliberation so that decisions can be arrived at. Deliberation and decision is foreign to a mind habituated to myths. A clever politician will therefore make allowances for those who prefer myths to facts – in the same way that someone who writes a contemporary novel will embroider truth with parable. Modern writers of novels, which is to say novelists, are just now discovering a hunger for truth because they are tiring – and I dare say their audience is tiring – of the exclusive multiplicity of myths, which really only caters to the fear of truth and in that way perpetuates modern crises. Let the politician realize that among his population are many who are fed up with the mere mythification of the political household but let him understand at the same time that a little magnanimity goes a long way.

*

We deal in myths when we do not think organically; when our interest in growth is not greater than our fear of truth. It is perfectly understandable that in the presence of someone who is mythically inclined and who is terrified of his self we should behave compassionately. If we ourselves have made a habit of perception, we have had help. If a child manages to become a contemporary adult he has had help. All the stages of our growth, however we view them, depend on cooperation with someone

36

in the next higher stage. A mature human being does not remain mature unless he turns compassionately towards the young and the immature. So we might say with certainty that as soon as we take an individualist stand we enter the department of myths and are to that extent then immersed in a story – or in history. We behave historically because we do not grow organically. *The* politician is a mythic entity just like the world is a mythic entity and we can – if we do not choose growth – exist in such quasi-supernatural states for years. If we take care not to let ourselves be bothered by those who behave in terms of growth – especially if we attack them and make them the butt of our criticism – we can persist for our lifetime as historic beings who think in terms of myths and have no life whatsoever.

Enough said, our politician will have to be able to recognize myths for what they are worth. They lend themselves to parable. However the only parable that makes helpful sense to the one who is unknowingly sustained by myths is the one that is com-passionately presented; he will be touched by it not provoca-tively but creatively. And in his case 'creatively' means in the direction of growth – even if only of growth as a possible no-tion or as a viable concept.

*

What we are reminded of here is the importance of a politi-cian getting to know his population. Is it largely a number of people whose mental furniture is mythic. In that case he will, to a degree at least, wish to stimulate them in the direction of growth. It is near impossible to govern people who are swayed overwhelmingly by myths except by force – unless one learns the skill of compassionate parable – of the story presented in kindly fashion and with relevance. The portion of the popula-tion that is able to think constructively will not be humiliated by such an approach, as it would be if the story, rather than compassionate, were insolent, condescending or critical. So there must be a great emphasis on the kindly approach if the psyche, hungry for myth, is to make room for fact and for a discussion of fact.

A section of the population may be tribal. This is where the myth of fortunate togetherness has taken hold and egotism of one sort or another is at any time liable to raise its ugly head. How can a politician best behave in that case, if his ambition is to govern? Will he confront? Will he seek to mollify, to make concessions, both to the tribe and its anti-tribe? An ego, after all, cannot exist by itself for long, it must have its anti-ego, to keep it heated.

The answer to this question of how a politician would best behave here is the same as in the case of a person who seeks to communicate, or have dealings of any sort, with an egotist. Since the egotist's central ambition, whatever else he puts forward or stirs up, is always to discover his anti-ego, the one who wishes to govern will have to pretend that this egotist is not really an egotist but a reasonable person – that this tribe, which makes up a portion of his population, is not really, or only superficially, a tribe and 'deep down' capable – and desirous – of reason and emotion. Once again, therefore, compassion will come into its own. Compassion does not preclude a sense of humour, for example. The difficulty always seems to be that while on one hand we realize how stupid it would be to confront an egotistic individual, at the same time we suppose that if we give in to him he will run circles around us. A politician's task, however, is not primarily to get along with people but to govern them, so he may have to step back from the egotist, or from the leader of the tribe – from the sheik – and give him room to exhibit himself in his finery. Sometimes there is a fine enough line between giving room and giving rope – to hang himself. The latter is not advisable because it breeds resentment.

*

A politician worth his salt gets to know his population and will try to come up, if necessary, with a multifaceted approach.

Overall, however, he will not seek to govern merely to keep the peace and to give everyone what he asks for but he will also encourage people to learn how to govern themselves. Only those who govern themselves grow. While we rely on others to govern us we do not grow but we stagnate and we arrogate. Arrogance and stagnation lead, respectively, to revolution and ill-being. Generally one imagines that principally excesses must be governed that there's an end of it. Keep the people in line. So mere government, or government in the absence of understanding and wisdom, is pointless and usually nothing but a case of 'asking for trouble', especially where a population has become accustomed to large portions of liberty.

So if organic growth rather than merely 'economic' or material growth is the aim, as it should be, a population will seek to 'govern itself'. Does that mean that politicians will become superfluous? No, it merely means that their role will change somewhat. A population is, after all, made up of individual people, and the more of them who learn how to govern themselves, the better. It's a matter of degree, once again. How does a politician know that renewed emphasis in the direction of self-government and growth is required? The crime rate rises. How do I maintain self-government once I have the knack of it ? I help others govern themselves. It's always the same. We keep what we have by sharing it. If we learn to think of democracy as self-government, we will be able to judge properly whether the population we are part of is indeed democratic and not just paying lip-service to an ideal taboo. How does a politician know that his population is ignorant of democracy? By the amount of street demonstration and public unrest. By how accusatively portions of it shout: Govern us? The desire to be governed is not childish but immature. The more mature we are, the less do we depend on others, such as politicians, to govern us.

*

A large portion of government activity is the business of the collective household. Let's not be too quick to accuse our politician of remission. Compare it to our own household. How orderly are we? How much of a mess do we make of our day merely because we do not discipline our minds sufficiently. How do we manage our money? Is our account usually overdrawn? Do we repair the fabric of the house in time? Do we share our equipment with our neighbours? Now lets compare this to how our politician gets on. He should have a fair notion of the state of the country. If he thinks in terms of household instead of pretending he is helping to run a corporation he is more likely to gain our respect. Very likely the modern race to keep up with the Joneses has him confused. And this is where the population is justified in applying pressure on its politician. Let those who have learned how to raise families and how to create a home rather than merely coexisting in a house, speak up in meetings, because that is how a politician learns what is required. He needs to keep in touch with the various communities so that he can think and feel communally rather than as a modern casualty. He will attend community meetings and make experimental contributions, to test the ground. He will take on board that a new generation of people is with us and among us, people who think differently from all generations before, and they have an inkling of contemporary community in their very blood. They were born with it. Their notion of good and evil is something altogether different.

*

The modern age, from which we are trying to distance ourselves even as we realize the extent to which we are still influenced by it, is under the control of two different evils, of two devils, if you like and we might just take a quick peek at those two malingerers. They both thrive on critical spirit, we have mentioned that many times, but this time I'd like to undertake a little analysis of them.

The two-thousand year old crisis can be described today, in short, as the undeniable urge to move on, contemporary with the ineluctable unwillingness to move on. That sums it up. From the modern point of view the 'moving on', therefore, is a blind urge, not otherwise to be described, partly because of the unwillingness to make sense of it. The urge is energetic, but it runs head on straight into the fear of the unknown and is frustrated. The tension of dynamic/inert prevails, with sporadic outbreaks from one side or the other. The dynamic is frustrated by fear of the unknown and inertia presents as malaise. The fear is combated religiously and scientifically and this results simultaneously in the original dynamic changing shape drastically until it is no longer recognizable as 'that which might, who knows under what sort of circumstances, be creatively utilized.' It makes little difference whether we look back on the religions and sciences as powered by fear or as misconceived urges. All we can say is that the urge to 'move on' was always available to courageous perception of truly creative impulse and that the fear was never so overpowering in itself that it might not have been faced in fundamental, human-natural faith. And this was, of course, done now and again during the modern age with more or less success. Today we look back on those attempts to 'move on' creatively and faithfully and we are full or admiration for those who managed it.

The modern response to the 'urge to move on' has not been a response at all but a reaction. Not until the time around the year 1968 has one been able to observe a world-wide expression of the modern tension as government versus people. Government is perceived by 'the people' as demonic while 'the population' is perceived by the government as chaotic. The struggle between the demonic and the chaotic indicates the demise of the modern age. What follows is not another age nor a period of any description but merely time taking place. We might enjoy thinking of it as the contemporary proposition and the fertile here and now, one or the other depending on whether we like to act or prefer to be.

It may help us to accommodate ourselves to the here and now if we imagine, in some lively manner, the two evils of modernity to which we still are prone. It is my contention that evil of any sort is merely evil in that it hides from us the face of god. So how do we approach evil? We ask ourselves: Why are we hiding the face of god? Why not look closely at the suspect energy input, such as the products of digital energy for but one example, and learn to distinguish between the tool and the use we make of it? And I consider that I speak to individual readers here and not to huge companies that service masses of investors in terms of buying power while betraying them by modifying their behaviour. I consider that I am, from beginning to end, responsible for myself and secondarily for my children and friends. My wife thinks the same, but from the feminine side. When I noticed, for example, that not only was I looking at more and more u-tube confections that glamorized animal violence but that in addition more and more violent confections were mysteriously being presented to me, I turned u-tube off. I recognized a failing in myself and gave myself time to think about things. I will probably never turn u-tube on again because, upon reflecting on how I felt while I serviced my lower instincts, I can say I am better off without it. Equally, while my children were growing out of their infancy I considered how television was influencing our communality, family and beyond, and spoke to my wife. We turned it off for a fortnight and observed. Marvellous changes. The set went into the skip. To be sure, I have not kept news of this beneficial change to myself but I have no evidence as yet that anyone benefited from the fact that I shared my experience.

So there we take note of this urgency to move on in ourselves and we have been informed that we are at liberty to both betray and abuse it. We are at liberty – not any longer to be modern, no, I don't think that's still possible, but maybe post-modern, in that the age, as it departs, trails clouds of mephitic odours. We may even notice, if we are honest with ourselves, that in addition to being at liberty we are actually liable to do so – namely to falsify this urge through misappropriation. Mephistopheles produces the stink. So we see double. The *dynamic demonic* goes into technology and the *chaotic dystopic* settles into government. We have the devil inside and the devil outside: two devils, the way we are caused to see it by our insistence on contemplating the mask we have pulled over the face of god rather than the face of god.

What great masses of heated conversation may be observed today from within the two camps of the dynamic demonic and the chaotic dystopic! However this is still post-modern. Eventually – unless we are very careful, and in consideration of the fact that every individual person has only so many years of energetic youthfulness during which he has what it takes to prepare himself not for adulthood only but for maturity – we run out of time before we can make he last adjustments to the limits and disciplines that will help us more and more to judge in the interest of urgent energy creatively shaped.

The last excuse always seems to be: Why, if it's good, isn't everybody doing it? Wouldn't it be interesting – and perhaps remarkably helpful – if along with every u-tube click came the notification that 'One-hundred and fifty-three people have only today turned this facility off again before using it' instead of: 'People who watched this also then watched this and this and the other'? That too could be classed as 'behaviour modification' but it might remind helpless minds.

Well, it's true, isn't it, that along with our primary responsibility for ourselves comes the secondary one for not misleading people. Government regulators are able to identify salesmen of snake-oil and of brushes that don't work, but what can they do to prevent demonic manipulation and dystopic organization? No data exist. Modern statistics do not apply. You either go with the sweet flow or you turn Facebook off. In German a 'Zuckerberg' is a sugar mountain. Americans pronounce it 'suckerberg'. Just saying.

However throwing stones instead of eating them is not enough. We have to get into the good habit of eating bread. And the use of the 'we' is often misleading in these cases, because one (one!) begins to sound like a majority of the adept. One imagines there must be a huge pool of population 'out there' that is fed up with behind-the-scenes manipulation of the innocents and more than ready to take that leap of faith (or of gullibility, depending on your point of view) into universal contemporary community. However there is probably every possible gradation from insanely involved to magically overextended too. Our imagination plays tricks on us if we picture it. The ethics of communality is one to two or three initially, then maybe to six or eight, but then it probably either runs dry or turns into something quite different, such as mass advertising or digital culture promotion.

What I have to ask myself is: How can I benefit from any enlightenment I gain when I see behind that mask. The demons chatter into my left ear and the dystopia appeals to my right eye. I imagine I will have to get busy with both hands. This is evil, I refuse to kid myself. It is evil not because some faceless monster delivers huge populations to the sword but because it presumes to be able to prevent me from evolving into a fully fledged contemporary person.

So here is what I do. I begin in a very small way to do something that is unmistakeably helpful to others and therefore to me. Giving money to others might seem to be helpful to them but it doesn't help me. I try to differentiate between the egocentric ethic and the communal ethic. Between a temporary feeling of self-righteousness and eternal emotion that heals. The demons clamour less insistently. Then I take a close look at the politicians I have helped to vote into position and try to get into the habit of thinking of them as people who need help. They need my help, because I as a citizen could not do without them and should therefore treat them with understanding and compassion. Will that not make them improve? I believe it will. I will speak to people who talk about politicians as if they were all scoundrels. Well, if they are, who voted for them? True enough, you say, but they were the best of the bunch. So I say: If you are so smart, then you should put your own self forward for selection to some office. Your reasons for not doing that might not be legitimate or honest.

Suddenly the dystopia looks less threatening. The government is taken over by some dictator? Well, I suggest you help to create a big vacuum around him so that he runs out of oxygen. Change the conditions that opened the door to a tyrannical ruler or a self-serving bureaucrat. A population of citizens of subjects is defined from the outside. Viewed from the inside they turn into a million or ten of persons who are all different. Some of them aren't even persons, but individuals who drift like a flock of starlings to where there is free food. They too have to be considered by the politician. Think of that before you slag him off.

*

What seems to be ever so difficult to grasp is that the modern and the communal exclude each other. There is a lot of talk about economic growth these days and of how it could be limited so as to make it less damaging. But unless we grow spiritually we do not have the wits to 'to keep the growth of the economy within sane limits'. And even that statement is slightly misleading because as soon as we grow spiritually, the economic growth takes care of itself. And only the economy that takes care of itself really works – as our household. I don't call home-making a control of the economy. The modern mind makes a thing out of homemaking and then those things mercifully draw pathological attention to themselves so that we will recognize we are

45

making a mistake. We are backing a lame horse. Next time let's put a lower bet on it? No, we will pick a different horse. Spiritual growth has to be learned. Sometimes a change of heart has to precede. Sometimes people repent of all the times they backed a lame horse, just generally, without making a hypocritical fuss. It clears the eye so that you see better.

Realizing that capitalism and economic growth are signs of a malaise amounts to the same as realizing that modernity is a malaise. However socialism and economic stagnation are also signs of a malaise and modern. Remember we mentioned that the modern tension of dynamic/inert prevails. Those who would replace capitalism with communism or socialism to cure the cancer of economic growth would substitute heart failure for cancer. Economic stagnation and economic growth, in terms of the modern malaise, amount to the same.

Spiritual growth commences like a seed in our nature and is thwarted and ignored in the name of modernity. This seed will not die and grow into a thriving and fruitful plant in terms of modern attitudes towards society and existence in the world but only on the basis of trust in merciful good spirit, in which case growth is not economic and neither does it stagnate but it may be furthered, cherished and understood in terms of developing thought, greater wisdom, a more compassionate attitude to neighbours, both persons and countries. It may readily and usefully be imagined as the essential vitality inherent in the growth of children as they are brought up, in the growth of adults as they develop towards maturity and followed by their evolution here and there as human beings with eternal life.

Economic growth, like economic stagnation, is therefore, by definition, a sidetrack of the modern existence in a finite world.

Even the expression 'economic growth' puts me off. It doesn't make sense. What kind of growth is it? It might be slow or quick, healthy or stunted, but how is it when it is economic? What about economical growth, when some live being makes good use of what it needs to grow? Growth is a natural process and I find it difficult to think of uneconomical growth. Equally, when I try to imagine what economic growth might be, if I don't accept the idea those terms stand for, not as decent language but as labels coined by professional students of how people behave, well, my mind boggles. Economic growth! No, it doesn't work. How can the management of a household grow?

But no wonder. When one tries to understand some modern language, especially as spoken by people who intellectualize and work for institutions, one is liable to get one's knickers in a twist. The Industrial Revolution is another oddity. Should it be the industrious revolution? But that's equally silly. How can we sensibly describe a revolution – given that we don't mean the revolution of a wheel? Certainly not as industrial. This is the modern way, the smacking of labels together like a magician bangs an apple together with a walnut and suddenly the walnut is in the apple. No explanation. The National Health! Not burgeoning or flagging but national – I ask you. The health of a nation, which one can at least imagine, should not be turned into national health.

As soon as we set out on our contemporary lives in our various communities, language makes sense again. Our brain is allowed to come into its own. How nice if politicians could speak to us in words, not labels! Some do, of course, and we are grateful to them.

*

Facing the fact that there is no material transition from modernity to contemporary communality, a politician would have to ask himself how he can possibly be asked to handle the various problems of too much and too little that stare him in the face. Even if he were to admit that economic growth, for but one example, is a misnomer and that a large number of the national ambitions, as he finds them on being elected, are misguided, how can he do some good – given that the only real good possible has to be in line with the unavoidable challenges of contemporary communality? Pretending that these challenges don't exist exacerbates the malaise – and he might be the only one who understands that. Realizing that in truth they do exist places him under immense ethical pressure. His dilemma is not different from the dilemma of the factory worker who is being asked to box faulty food for quick profit and consumption. They would both like to keep the job but not under any and all circumstances. The work has to make sense before he is willing to continue with it, wage or no wage.

Nothing remains for our politician but to search within himself for any remnants of modernism that prevent him from detecting an ethical way forward. We have already indicated the sort of thing he is liable to find there. We have mentioned the peculiar duality that indicates the end-time of the modern age and at the same time the challenge of what is on its way and what will automatically meet with catastrophe unless it is approached as a blessing.

Getting stuck in the mutual contradiction of the demonic and the chaotic is the typical recipe for catastrophe both left and right. This contradiction is, of course, played out in the open, however it commences in individuals and has to be resolved by those individual persons. Our politician will find his own language, no doubt, for this contradiction in himself. All we can do here is describe the sort of thing he is bound to find. There is the energetic urge to do, to be seen to be 'making things happen'. Against that there is the fear of consequences. Every intended act – that is to say, the intention of every mechanically contrived act – right away seems to activate a panic – a panic which, in his desperation, he will feel pressed either to overcome or to lie down under. In other words, both acting and refraining from acting appear equally drastic, equally fraught with risk and failure. If he is worth his salt he will gradually acquire the skill of holding out. He will hold out not in spite of what he finds himself to be up against but because he has learned and hopefully at least partly understands that holding out under that pressure achieves something. Intelligence, for example, is what accumulates and specifically the intelligence required for moving on, moving forward, towards and into contemporary communality. It occurs to him what to do and he marvels that in no way is it anything that he might have arrived at by acting rashly or by a cowardly refraining from acting.

Does it surprise us that a politician should be truly creative? How sad that it should surprise us!

*

What I have described as the undeniable urge to move on simultaneous (contemporary?) with the ineluctable unwillingness or reluctance to move on is, technically speaking, a postmodern phenomenon. In public we are no longer willing to blunder ahead rashly or able to fool ourselves that our unwillingness to act is every time a case of wise caution. The doubts that are setting in – and that are being analyzed – in relation to 'economic growth' for example – are being faced in earnest, as the various published monographs show.

As to criticism of recent developments on the world stage, this can be show to be pointless because whatever has been done can be used as a stepping stone for moving on. Criticism gets us bogged down in the modern world. Both the formation of the European Community and the unwillingness of a slim majority of British voters to continue to play that game can be understood as transition phenomena, in which case the next move will be less hampered by shame and blame, which does nothing for creative growth. We may train ourselves in magnanimity. From the modern point of view, both the modern historic past and the modern philosophic future are systematic if only one keeps at it, while to us they are locked boxes and no one is bothered looking for the key.

However, as I say, the modern point of view is being challenged, both by the spirit of the time and by those among us who are capable of contemporary communality. Politicians who get together, in twos and threes, to converse honestly about the dynamic/inertia tension they might be experiencing, who are willing to confess to this tendency to react, rather than to respond, to the contemporary challenges and who are aware of the tragic discrepancy between the politicians' perception of the population as chaotic and of the population's perception of politicians as demonic – such politicians decidedly have the edge. In other words, where two or three get together in the name of contemporary communality, there the creative decision originates.

Some democratic politicians know about this, of course, and they can see why the acting upon such original, creative decisions does not necessarily imply a cessation of democratic party politics right away. The outward forms of the old never need to be destroyed, or 'deconstructed', because they will fade in their own time in the light of the shape of what is to come. What does play into the hands of disruption and chaos is not disloyalty to party but disloyalty to truth – and truth is nothing to be afraid of. Truth in itself is gentle and mild, is meek and kindly, is willing even to efface itself for the greater good, and much more in that vein. However truth will be confessed. It reaches into the soul from both sides, from body and mind, and if outwardly we do not mean it we have no inward satisfaction of it. If politicians are not truthful to one another they will, whether they want to or not, play into the hands of chaos in public. And chaos is not pretty. Eventually heads role, metaphorically or in the light of day, and nothing is gained by that. On the contrary. People merely distance themselves from government and leave the demagogues a free hand, as the calamity proceeds.

It's a mistake to think of the population as passive and weak. Evil is a distinct possibility in the heart of every individual voter. And evil is ready to be active or passive. It readily switches from one to the other to remind us of our modern duplicity – or nowadays, more appropriately, of our susceptibility to modern duplicity. And shying away from evil is as sickening in the long run as resisting evil is damaging in the short run. If a politician is not able and willing to stand on his own two feet he will soon lose sight of this.

*

The population of the earth is a concept that lends itself readily nowadays to our contemplation as a number of communities that are more or less willing to reveal themselves as communal rather than as national. I believe if one cared to look one would come across great numbers of individual people who do not feel the need to be dominated by political cliques but who see the need for a kind of committee that will realize the popular consensus. A population welcomes leaders but broadly speaking they must be more intelligent and wise than the population. What happens all too often is that the public sees individuals in government office with whom one would not be able to sit down for a conversation, for a variety of reasons. Intelligence and wisdom do not often stand out. So what does it take to establish the consensus? Something like a foreman, I suppose. Someone who will collect the money and then hire the builders and oversee them. A foreman sees no need to practice public speaking and he will never ask: How the hell are we going to present this idea to the people? One mistake and we're out of power. Really a foreman has no such power.

The divide between public and private, between popular and esoteric, between politicians and populations, between rulers and the ruled – is modern and is being 'found out'. The tendency is cosmic. Which means that we expect to come across numbers of phenomena that show what happens when the trend is allowed to happen and not creatively comprehended and worked out. For those who have no notion of the contemporary spirit, these public phenomena will be as puzzling and startling, if not seriously disturbing, as the number of young people who commit suicide, as the increasing indistinctness of gender or the popular appeal of nonentities who have nothing going for them except a lack of arrogance. By the public phenomena that indicate how the contemporary spirit must appear if it is neither realized creatively nor even welcome or understood I mean everything that smacks of international world domination. Do we really suppose that mega-corporations will be checked by a modern political will? A single politician who faces up, in himself, to the dynamic/inert tension and perhaps joins up with two or three others who do the same, all of whom are aware of the demonic-chaotic, post-modern psychosis and seek to arrive at creative insights into how to 'move on' into contemporary communality – such single politicians and small groups of politicians can make moves that will disconcert the entire post-modern circus. One of the secrets here is to maintain trust in what has the sense to remain small.

*

When political decision are made in terms of society and not of community, what happens is that large-scale investment in survival values uses up the energy that has no time, consequently, to become available to individual people.

By investment in survival values I mean all those decisions that would help us to live longer with no attention paid to any effect such decision might have on life.

Society is itself a survival strategy. Survival of the fittest, as a concept, sums up modern society. The question is, to what extent does a politician nowadays still have to keep society, and societies, in the forefront of his mind; perhaps out of sense of duty? Certainly the population of the earth cannot be imagined in terms of a collection of societies, nor would the average person nowadays insist that he must be computed as a social being. Society places constraints and exacts tribute, while people by and large seem to have better things in mind.

Survival of the fittest is capitalism. It will always appeal to those who cannot wait to impress themselves upon the world rather than living in it. As a capitalist one removes or subtracts oneself from the world and begins to manipulate the so-called affairs of the world, from outside. One begins to suffer from demonic aggression and secretly hopes to be able to ignore laws other than the ones one invents to service one's interests. 'Demonic', by the way, means 'spiritually tied up in the red tape of the psyche'. The Free Market is the stomping-ground of the demons. Demons are spirits that inhabit available bodies. If a man with a soul encounters a capitalist, he first collapses a little inwardly and then insists on character and personality. This allows him to withstand the demonic infection. On account of his removal of himself from the world, the capitalist is incapable of compassion and as a direct consequence his spiritual growth dries up. One comes across capitalists who, with the demeanour of naïve children, commit atrocities in total innocence and ignorance of moral consequence. In the absence of spiritual growth, a capitalist must insist on material growth and it turns materialist as even his psyche turns threadbare. However one of the effects of unrecognized spirit of contemporary communality, as it moves in, so to speak, is a hollowing out of all such natures, to the point where they can no longer make practical decisions or sustain the pressures of the need to survive. So once again, the gas will escape in due time from this phenomenon called capitalism and there is no need to fight it. And Socialism in the meantime collapses under its own weight.

*

Survival of the fittest – here the thinking individual right away asks: Fittest for what? A peculiar concept, surely. When you're fit you fit in – but into what? It depends on the context. One thing is for certain, you can fit into development but not into evolution. Actually fitness may be the decisive factor when we compare development with evolution, or vice versa.

Development is orderly. It has to be, to get from A to B. We speak of a plan, of a pattern and of a design. We might go so far as to mention a system, so that we can envision the entire collection of parts together as one. And then we start to panic. Is it a closed system? If so, I want out.

Our politician opens his eyes – wide. As soon as we mentioned the possibility of that closed system he sensed danger. He sensed epidemic and revolution. He feels strangely and intensely addressed in his sense of himself as a public servant. Is this the time perhaps for him to acquaint himself with what happens to the body politic when it becomes systematic? Because that would mean that the door is closed and locked between development and evolution. The moderns are forever developing, aren't they. There is the developed and the undeveloped and even the under-developed world. We might even look into it being overdeveloped. Anyhow, development becomes the modern end in itself. We try to imagine, we moderns, what the end is of development and all we can think of is better this and more of that.

The developing world supposedly gets richer, healthier, happier but its all a matter of degree and no end in sight. Is that how far our politician wants to look? If so, then we have no further interest in him because he is on his way out. Surely, he remonstrates, that is my limit? What else do you expect from me? Even the stable state and the powerful nation go no further than that? Are you maybe a troublemaker? Are we going to have to take a peek at your emails?

There you go. You see what I mean, don't you. The modern world as a closed system. The Nation, Society, the Family – all closed systems – and beyond 'there be demons'.

Ah no, excuse me, that is a common mistake, if I may be so bold as to point it out. The demons are not beyond, they are not outside the guarded border of the enclosed Nation, Society,

Family but inside. They are the ones who for their collective demonic comfort and convenience shut themselves in – and us along with them. So when a politician looks at his job sheet, right near the top it should say: Open the door!

Yes, open the door. Start with that. By no means should you start a fight with the demons. Don't try to mediate or compromise with them either. If you don't know what I mean by the demons, go to the door and rattle the doorknob. Pretend you might be thinking about opening – and there they are. At the start they are very nice about it. You are deluded, they will tell you, in the most humanist, liberalist fashion. You see, they will inform you kindly, you are about to do something you will regret. Oh yes. Others have tried and history has not been kind to them.

The thing is, if you were to smile, to open the door and to step out into evolution, that would be the last you would hear of them. They are the guardians of the closed system and I dare say they have their uses – because only those who come up with the courage are meant to evolve. Survival of the fittest in that closed system and then evolution of the liveliest.

*

The politician we have in mind does not take kindly to my description of the finite world and I don't blame him. What's all this business about demons, he wants to know. I am perfectly well aware of where my work starts and where it has to end. The evolving human being governs him- or herself and therefore doesn't require my services. He has no wish, no tendency even, to go against the law and it would never occur to him to interfere with others, to tell them what to do and what to avoid doing. He sets examples, makes the odd suggestion and generally offers help to those who seem to need it. He is well behaved and good to have as company. You might say that his contributions to mankind are cultural, but there's more to it. Those who need me are the ones who are stuck in their development. There, that's all you need to say. They are stuck, they try to get others stuck for company and they don't realize they're stuck, most of the time. They are modern throughout. All I have to do is make sure I don't get stuck along with them. I am an artist of sorts and I can be a good artist or a bad artist. I can hold out a mirror to 'modern man' and leave it at that. I can go through all the motions of politics as my career, take pains to be an upstanding member of Society and draw my salary at the end of the month. Now and again I will say something that gets in the papers but mostly I play it safe. However there are those who expect more than that from me and nowadays there are a lot of them. During the last fifty years young people have woken up, so it seems. They are not impressed by any pontificating. They can see further than most adults, strangely enough. And whenever I ask myself what, in conscience, might be my considered contribution to the young, I always, eventually, come around to the following: They need to be shown that the so-called system is open-ended for those who have what it takes. And that's the trick, as I see it, that it's not enough for me to talk about it but they need to be shown. The time has come, the Walrus said, not to speak of dreams but to show them.

And that is where the personality of the politician comes into its own. If he is 'like a politician' he doesn't have a hope. Some of the population looks for that, I suppose, because they are wedded to the status quo but the young look right through it and what they see is not the politician but the individual person. Who is this guy? they say. What is he up to? What can he do? Those are the questions they ask. They have good eyesight, so there's no need for him to be demonstrative, flamboyant, charismatic. That only puts them off. He can be a lord or a labourer, but he has to be genuine. He has to have something to say and when he says it he has to mean it. In short, he has to realize, to know and understand, that nowadays evolution is not only possible but mandatory. We either evolve or dissolve.

*

When have you last seen a politician who said he was sorry but he made a mistake? Are politicians not allowed to make mistakes? I suppose one would need to talk about what it means to make a mistake. Let's face it, everything works out somehow. And if we pretend that it's all part of a master plan to which we alone are privy, well, who can gainsay us? However, what if all of modern politics were one big mistake because human life is really not suited to systematic decision-making? Until we realize that evolutionary growth must be part of our everyday existence and while we insist that *this* system rather than *that* system is the one and only true one, all the planning we do and the policies we devise bring us no closer to the only thing that works, which is whatever aids and abets communal growth – which is the growth of every member of the community. Children grow up. Adults grow in maturity. In sum, this is what we mean by communal growth. Democracy is a word. If we think of it as opposed to other methods of government we mean something different. In any case, while our main concern is our rights, we live in a dark age, whatever the date. Growth is development and evolution. Can it make any sense at all that we speak of the growth of a community? Well, yes, we can imagine a thriving community in comparison to one that is not thriving. We might need to get down to brass tacks here and speak of a particular population that is thriving, or at least aiming to thrive, within given and chosen geographic parameters, such as near an estuary, in a fertile valley, within reach of an oasis. This is the way settlements take root in any case, when people imagine they can make a go of it somewhere as long as they're left in peace for a while. A fishing village develops. In the valley they grow grapes. In the desert they hunt the gnu, that sort of thing. They acquire various skills that pertain to their lifestyle.

Now they look around. Who else is making a go of it? Let's introduce ourselves. We will bring gifts.

This goes on variously on the earth, of course. And the elements, harsh or clement, make people think. We learn how to cope with the changes in temperature, with the seasons and the weather. We learn how to communicate with other communities. If we come across a population that finds itself at a very early stage of communal development, compared to our own, we might show them a few of our own tricks. There is no reason, in a community, to separate survival out from life. This may sound like a remarkable discovery at the moment, when we have been lured into all the modern survival theories at the expense of life.

This has to be recognized as soon as possible, if we intend to speak meaningfully of contemporary community, namely that **survival is not separate from life**. The separation is a modern one and it had to be made so that we would learn to appreciate the marriage of the two as one. The modern individual has a job or a career so that he can earn his money and survive. When he comes home he tries to 'live a little'. But let's face it, it's not real life, life in truth, is it. It's a pretend thing, a substitute, tied to what he can afford, the electricity for next month, a cruise maybe, this year, or an extension to his private island because without his own airstrip, come on, you're not living, are you? The modern standard of living is really a standard of survival. But let's not go on about it. The point is, that for a thriving contemporary community there is growth in terms of development and evolution, and this appertains equally to the members of the community and to the community itself. We might go so far as to say that the member of the community is the community, if only to get this picture of a group of people at loose ends out of our mind. It does pertain to our image here that a politician is bound to have a head full of modern sociology and modern anthropology not to mention modern political science, economics and law, that would persuade him to think of 'his' population as a number of nonentities that require the shaping hand in order to become communal. Some Christian missionaries regard their 'primitive tribes' like that, I dare say, as lost in confusion, just waiting for the supernatural blessing and the Old Testament education. In consideration of where we find ourselves at this moment, while the change of all changes is going on, with us or without us, we do have to participate in the change ourselves, even though – or perhaps especially if – we feel we have what it takes to be politicians. Only consider that we may still be members of a political party, for goodness sakes, and that in one particular direction we really have to play a bit of a game so as not to rub traditionalists up the wrong way while we make our more enlightened moves. We may find ourselves moving in and out of party politics and never mind how that is perceived by others.

We might define a contemporary politician at this stage as anyone who rightly feels that he has what it takes to be responsible for a community population. That community population may be in its very early stages and he himself may still be participating in modern politics. We can be sure that as soon as a group or a number of people identify themselves as a true community they have something else in mind and equally as soon as someone identifies himself as the leader, say, of a true community, he himself, like the people he identifies with or represents, is not contemporary. Since every contemporary community is open-ended, so must every contemporary politician be open-minded – open spirited, really. We all love to gather round a celebrity and to identify with labels but that is modern. What ever we do or leave undone in the name of anything but the truth is not contemporary. Writers want to sell their books, that is understandable, but as soon as they set sail by hoisting some formula that will identify them in the future – a flag around which devoted followers will gather – they are heading for the storm or the doldrums. As soon as we want to be good because we follow some particular leader we are worse than usual.

Even those who tell us they believe in and follow Jesus would be smarter to just do it and keep quiet about it. That way the truth has a chance of bearing fruit. Blazon it on high and thought dries up. Never forget that the political environment in which we find ourselves is still attached to a degree of modern thinking, which in its latest fading stages would offer us, in a word, international bliss. An abuse of otherwise useful techniques (technologies?) would steer us in that direction. The techniques are useful in that we may hear of one another, not so that we may manipulate others and intrude into their lives.

This would suggest to me that contemporary politicians as such will gradually become less necessary. In other words, as a contemporary community thrives, what will happen, just as it does in the case of a mature person, is that something new and strange will occur and precisely at that time – and for that time – people will then to look to someone who has the political gift. They will not set him on a pedestal so that they can tear him down again once all seems to be well. He may not even be the same man they looked to last time to help them figure out what is going on. What counts, when all else is said and done, is that awareness of being communal is kept alive. It is an awareness on which one must be able to count. Communal awareness is what it all comes down to – not that we are members of a community or what our community is called or who is the leader of it, or what its 'cause' is by which it identifies itself, and so on. Every individual person wishes and needs to have this contemporary awareness of himself and herself in community, because that is how we develop and evolve, how we grow – how we thrive.

* * *

60

www.ingramcontent.com/pod-product-compliance
Lightning Source LLC
Chambersburg PA
CBHW061733250726
48657CB00002B/904